Su...

of

House of Trump, House of Putin
Craig Unger

Conversation Starters

By Paul Adams
Book Habits

Bonus Downloads
*Get Free Books with **Any Purchase** of* Conversation Starters!

Every purchase comes with a FREE download!

Add spice to any conversation
Never run out of things to say
Spend time with those you love

Get it Now

or Click Here.

Scan Your Phone

Tips for Using Conversation Starters:

EVERY GOOD BOOK CONTAINS A WORLD FAR DEEPER THAN the surface of its pages. Questions herein are designed to bring us beneath the surface of the page and invite us into the world that lives on. These questions can be used to:

- Foster a deeper understanding of the book
- Promote an atmosphere of discussion for groups
- Assist in the study of the book, either individually or corporately
- Explore unseen realms of the book as never seen before

Table of Contents

Introducing *House of Trump, House of Putin*

ouse of Trump, House of Putin: The Untold Story of Donald Trump and the Russian Mafia is a book written by Craig Unger. It investigates the links that bind Donald Trump, Vladimir Putin, and the Russian Mafia and how this led to Trump's winning the US presidency.

Unger starts his investigation back in the 1970s when the previously unknown real estate businessman Donald Trump surfaces in New York and ends with the man being inaugurated into the office of the US President. The Trump presidency is the culmination of Russian president Vladimir Putin's secret work. Putin and his oligarchs spent many years burrowing into the foundation of American democracy. He had the Russian Mafia and oligarchs to assist him in this. Some twenty years ago, the Russians came to Trump's aid when his Atlantic City hotel and casino businesses went through massive failures.

The book reveals how the Cold War never really ended but evolved into a different phase. Trump's apartments became the means through which billions of dollars left the Soviet Union. The author mines the hidden alliance between Americans and the Russian Mafia. He uncovers how Russia regained its power after the Cold War and how it never stopped attacking the West. Trump was a key factor in the Russian covert effort to regain its superpower status. He would not be president today if Russia did not work behind the scenes to support him. The book explains how superpowers play their game behind the scenes. Key personalities like Michael Cohen, Paul Manafort, and Felix Sater are mentioned in the book.

Part of Unger's research is his look into nightclubs, resorts, restaurants, and other establishments visited by criminals and oligarchs of Russian origins. These tours are shown to end up in the White House as well as in the Trump Tower. Critics say that this is clear that Putin and Russian money has enabled Trump's political career. The author interviews and quotes intelligence authorities like Glenn Carle who worked as an intelligence officer for the CIA, and James Comey, former FBI director. Carle is cited as saying he thinks "Trump is actually working directly for the Russians." Comey relates the dinner he had with Trump at the White House, just before Trump fired him. Trump reportedly demanded loyalty from Comey, just like a Mafia boss does. Unger quotes Comey in the latter's book *A Higher Loyalty*. Comey says listening to Trump talk like the Mafia left him shaken; he has "never seen anything like it in the Oval Office." The author also quotes James Clapper former intelligence head who says Trump is an "intelligence asset" serving the Russians. The book traces Trump's links with a convict, Felix Sater, who is known to work with Russian members of the Mafia. Trump reportedly did not declare Sater's criminal background. Unger's research shows Trump was deep in debt, amounting to as much as $4 billion when the Russians rescued him. Indebted to them, it was Russian money that helped him recover from an almost failed business, thus leading to his political ascent. The book does not only implicate Trump but other Republicans and Democrats as well, who accepted millions of dollars of Russian money through private individuals or companies. Senator Mitch McConnell has such Russian ties going for twenty years now. Even FBI heads and counsel Mitchell Rogovin, Louis Freeh and William Sessions have questionable ties with the Russians.

The book provides two narrative strands of Trump and Putin, telling stories about the two heads of the world's two most powerful nations. The narratives alternate as the book progresses. One half of the book tells Trump's rise as a businessman using dirty money, while the other half paints a portrait of Semion Mogilevich, a mafia boss, and Putin's ascent to power. The story of how collusion between the two leaders is built up by the author. Trump's first time to visit Moscow in the 1980's is told. This is followed by accounts of suspicious meetings between a Russian ambassador and Trump's election team. A similarly strange meeting is recounted between a Russian lawyer and Donald Trump Jr. at the Trump Tower. Critics cite the book's well-researched information. Unger's sources are well-documented. Other critics, however, think that the book does not offer new information.

The book's strength is reportedly found in the way the author stitches together available information and recent developments in the investigation being done on Trump's alleged collusion by independent counsel Robert Mueller. The book is composed of 20 chapters ending with a list of the 59 connections with Russia that Trump allegedly forged over the past decades. Photographs are included in the book serving as a visual supplement to the author's research.

House of Trump, House of Putin is written by Unger who is best known for his *New York Times* bestselling *House of Bush, House of Saud*.

Discussion Questions

"Get Ready to Enter a New World"

Tip: Begin with questions dealing with broader issues to ensure ample time for quality discussions. Read through all discussion questions before engaging.

question 1

Unger starts his investigation back in the 1970s when the previously unknown real estate businessman Donald Trump surfaces in New York and ends with the man being inaugurated into the office of the US President. How did Trump start his real estate business?

~~~

question 2

The Trump presidency is the culmination of Russian president Vladimir Putin's secret work. How many years did Putin and the Russian mafia spend working on Trump? How did they cultivate him?

~~~

~~~

question 3

Putin and his oligarchs spent many years burrowing into the foundation of American democracy. Why does Russia want to undermine American democracy?

~~~

~~~

question 4

The Russians came to Trump's aid when his Atlantic City hotel and casino businesses went through massive failures. How did they help him?

~~~

question 5

The Cold War never really ended but evolved into a different phase. The book uncovers how Russia regained its power after the Cold War and how it never stopped attacking the West. How does the author prove this assertion?

~~~

question 6

Key personalities like Michael Cohen, Paul Manafort, and Felix Sater are mentioned in the book. Who are these people and how are they implicated?

~~~

~~~

question 7

Part of Unger's research is his look into nightclubs, resorts, restaurants, and other establishments visited by criminals and oligarchs of Russian origins. Why do the Russians frequent these places?

~~~

~ ~ ~

question 8

The author interviews and quotes intelligence authorities like Glenn Carle who worked as an intelligence officer for the CIA, and James Comey, former FBI director. What do these men think about Trump?

~ ~ ~

~~~

question 9

The book provides two narrative strands of Trump and Putin. One half of the book tells about Trump's rise as a businessman. What is the other half of the book composed of?

~~~

question 10

The story of how collusion between the two leaders is built up by the author. Trump's first time to visit Moscow in the 1980's is told. What other events led to the collision?

question 11

Critics cite the book's well-researched information. Unger's sources are well-documented. What sources were identified by Unger? Are these credible sources?

~~~

question 12

The book's strength is reportedly found in the way the author stitches together available information and recent developments in the investigation being done on Trump's alleged collusion. Do you like the way the author stitched the information together? How did he do this?

~~~

~~~

question 13

The book is composed of 20 chapters ending with a
list of the 59 connections with Russia that Trump
allegedly forged over the past decades. Do you
think the book is exhaustive of the subject? Why?
Why not?

~~~

~~~

question 14

Photographs are included in the book serving as a
visual supplement to the author's research.
Do the photos help support the author's claims?
Why? Why not?

~~~

question 15

The book does not only implicate Trump but other Republicans and Democrats as well, who accepted millions of dollars of Russian money through private individuals or companies. Who are these people identified by Unger? How are they implicated?

~~~

question 16

The Guardian says the book's conclusion is unsatisfying. The answers to important questions are not found and "Unger does little to add to our knowledge." Do you think the review has a point? Why? Why not?

~~~

~~~

question 17

The New York Times review says the book is an "explosive work of journalism." What makes the work explosive? Do you think this book will have a disrupting effect among readers? Why? Why not?

~~~

~~~

question 18

The Atlanta Journal-Constitution says the book "builds a momentum and discovery that makes it impossible to stop reading." Did you feel the momentum while reading the book? What makes it hard to stop reading?

~~~

question 19

Newsday review says Unger's previous book House of Bush, House of Saud was an act of public service that makes readers see the problem and demand accounting. Can this be said the same of his latest book? How similar are the two books?

~~~

~~~

question 20

Spectator USA says Unger's research shows how Trump's Russian connections end up in the White House as well as in the Trump Tower. Do you think the author made a clear case for the collusion between Putin and Trump? Why? Why not?

~~~

Introducing the Author

Craig Unger authored House of Bush, House of Saud: The Secret Relationship Between the World's Two Most Powerful Dynasties. The book, published in 2004, investigates the deep connections between the Bush family and Saudi Arabia's Royal Family. Unger claims in the book that 30 years ago, business deals between these two families were established which unintentionally led to today's terrorism and wars. The Bush family entered into deals with the Royal Family that allowed them access to oil. In exchange, the Royal Family were provided military protection and lucrative investments. Unger calls the two families "the world's two most powerful dynasties" whose ties support America's enemies. He posed the question to his readers, of President Bush having a role in the evacuation of Saudi Arabians following the 9/11 tragedy. He says the Saudi family reportedly had $1.4 billion in investments sunk into the Bush family's businesses. This book is the basis of the 2004 documentary film Fahrenheit 9/11 directed by Michael Moore.

In an article he wrote for The Guardian dated September 11, 2004, Unger said: "Bush is actually soft on terror." He does not truly want to go after the terrorists who caused 9/11 because he shielded the Saudis from being implicated. The Saudis are known to fund the al-Qaida. Bush allegedly obstructed any investigations focusing on them.

Unger, formerly the deputy editor The New York Observer, also wrote The Fall of the House of Bush published in 2007. The book is about the internal clashes within the Bush family and how the conservative Christian movement colluded with the Republican party. Unger presents the beliefs and worldviews of both groups and how the alliance affects American policy in a negative and undemocratic manner.

Unger was Boston Magazine's editor-in-chief, and also wrote for New York Magazine, Vanity Fair, The New Yorker, and Esquire. He co-wrote the 2016 book When Women Win: Emily's List and the Rise of Women in American Politics. The book tells the story of women elected into office over the past century. The founder of Emily's List is featured, showing how this influential group of women entered the political landscape. The group's founder, Ellen R. Malcolm, established the organization in 1985 to get women involved in politics. The organization worked to have women leaders elected into office including 19 senators and 11 governors. Hillary Clinton, Tammy Baldwin, and Nancy Pelosi are among the women leaders interviewed in the book. Boss Rove: Inside Karl Rove's Secret Kingdom of Power was published by Unger in 2014. It tells the story of Karl Rove, the mastermind behind George

W. Bush's political career. Unger describes the man as a "brilliant political operator," a man who is deemed dangerous to America and its democratic ideals.

Unger is often sought out as a speaker on political issues for shows in CNN, MSNBC, and the ABC Radio Network. He studied at Harvard University and is a resident of New York City.

Bonus Downloads
*Get Free Books with **Any Purchase** of* Conversation Starters!

 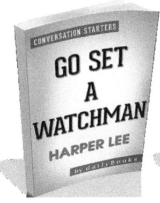 

Every purchase comes with a FREE download!

Add spice to any conversation
Never run out of things to say
Spend time with those you love

Get it Now

or Click Here.

Scan Your Phone

Fireside Questions

"What would you do?"

Tip: These questions can be a fun exercise as it spurs creativity among the readers by allowing alternate scene endings and "if this was you" questions.

question 21

Craig Unger authored House of Bush, House of Saud: The Secret Relationship Between the World's Two Most Powerful Dynasties. The book, published in 2004, investigates the deep connections between the Bush family and Saudi Arabia's Royal Family. How does he portray the Bush family in this book?

~~~

question 22

He says the Saudi family reportedly had $1.4 billion in investments sunk into the Bush family's businesses. House of Bush is the basis of the 2004 documentary film Fahrenheit 9/11 directed by Michael Moore. Have you seen the film? How was Unger's research reflected in the film?

~~~

question 23

He also wrote The Fall of the House of Bush published in 2007. The book is about the internal clashes within the Bush family and how the conservative Christian movement colluded with the Republican party. What are the interesting revelations he wrote about the Christian groups in this book?

question 24

He co-wrote the 2016 book When Women Win: Emily's List and the Rise of Women in American Politics. The book tells the story of women elected into office over the past century. What is Emily's List? How did it influence American politics?

~~~

question 25

It tells the story of Karl Rove, the mastermind behind George W. Bush's political career. Unger describes the man as a "brilliant political operator," a man who is deemed dangerous to America and its democratic ideals. Why is Rove dangerous to America? Do you agree with Unger?

question 26

The book provides two narrative strands of Trump and Putin, telling stories about the two heads of the world's two most powerful nations. The narratives alternate as the book progresses. If you are to reorder the chapters in the book to make it more interesting, how would you do it? Why?

~~~

question 27

The book is composed of 20 chapters ending with a list of the 59 connections with Russia that Trump allegedly forged over the past decades. If you are to compress all this information into a slimmer book, how would you do it? What parts will you remove?

~~~

question 28

Photographs are included in the book, serving as a visual supplement to the author's research. If illustrations are added in the book, what kind would you suggest? Why?

~ ~ ~

question 29

He co-wrote the 2016 book When Women Win: Emily's List and the Rise of Women in American Politics. The book tells the story of women elected into office over the past century. If he is to write another book about women and politics what subject would you want him to write about? Why?

~ ~ ~

question 30

Boss Rove: Inside Karl Rove's Secret Kingdom of Power was published by Unger in 2014. It tells the story of Karl Rove, the mastermind behind George W. Bush's political career. If he is to write another book about a figure who worked behind a president, who would you suggest? Why?

Quiz Questions

"Ready to Announce the Winners?"

Tip: Create a leaderboard and track scores to see who gets the most correct answers. Winners required. Prizes optional.

quiz question 1

The book reveals how the _____ War never really ended but evolved into a different phase. He uncovers how Russia regained its power and how it never stopped attacking the West.

quiz question 2

Unger quotes from the book A Higher Loyalty. Former FBI director _____ says listening to Trump talk like the Mafia left him shaken; he has "never seen anything like it in the Oval Office."

quiz question 3

Unger's research shows Trump was deep in debt, amounting to as much as _____ when the Russians rescued him. Indebted to them, it was Russian money that helped him recover from an almost failed business.

quiz question 4

True or False: The book does not only implicate Trump but other Republicans and Democrats as well, who accepted millions of dollars of Russian money through private individuals or companies.

~~~

quiz question 5

True or False: The book's strength is found in the way the author stitches together available information and recent developments in the investigation being done on Trump's alleged collusion by independent counsel Robert Mueller.

~~~

quiz question 6

True or False: The book is composed of 10 chapters ending with a list of the 70 connections with Russia that Trump allegedly forged over the past decades.

~~~

quiz question 7

True or False: Photographs are included in the book serving as a visual supplement to the author's research.

~~~

quiz question 8

Craig Unger authored _____.It investigates the deep connections between the Bush family and Saudi Arabia's Royal Family.

~~~

quiz question 9

He also wrote _____published in 2007. The book is about the internal clashes within the Bush family and how the conservative Christian movement colluded with the Republican party.

quiz question 10

True or False: He co-wrote the 2016 book When Women Win: Emily's List and the Rise of Women in American Politics.

quiz question 11

True or False: Boss Rove: Inside Karl Rove's Secret Kingdom of Power was published by Unger in 2014. It tells the story of Karl Rove, the mastermind behind George W. Bush's political career.

~ ~ ~

quiz question 12

True or False: He studied at Harvard University and is a resident of San Francisco.

~ ~ ~

Quiz Answers

1. Cold
2. Comey
3. $4 billion
4. True
5. True
6. False
7. True
8. House of Bush
9. The Fall of the House of Bush
10. True
11. True
12. False

Ways to Continue Your Reading

E VERY month, our team runs through a wide selection of books to pick the best titles for readers and reading groups, and promotes these titles to our thousands of readers – sometimes with free downloads, sale dates, and additional brochures.

Click here to sign up for these benefits.

If you have not yet read the original work or would like to read it again, you can purchase the original book here.

Bonus Downloads
*Get Free Books with **Any Purchase** of* Conversation Starters!

Every purchase comes with a FREE download!

Add spice to any conversation
Never run out of things to say
Spend time with those you love

Scan Your Phone

On the Next Page...

If you found this book helpful to your discussions and rate it a 4 or 5, please write us a review on the next page.

Any length would be fine but we'd appreciate hearing you more! We'd be very encouraged.

Till next time,

BookHabits

"Loving Books is Actually a Habit"

CPSIA information can be obtained
at www.ICGtesting.com
Printed in the USA
BVHW072313311019
562665BV00002B/307/P

9 780464 782742